The Beatles

A LIFE IN PICTURES

The Beatles

A LIFE IN PICTURES

TIM HILL

BARNES
&NOBLE
BOOKS
NEW YORK

A BARNES & NOBLE BOOK

©2004 by Barnes & Noble Publishing, Inc.

ISBN 0-7607-5613-9

All photographs ©Associated Newspapers Ltd. except
©Bettman/Corbis: pp. 9, 11, 26 top , 27 top, 32, 35, 45 top, 51 top , 65 top, 72 bottom, 94
©GettyImages: p. 13

Produced by Atlantic Publishing

Printed and bound in China by SNP Leefung Printers Limited

3 5 7 9 10 8 6 4 2

Dedication

For Laura and Jenny

Acknowledgments

Particular thanks to Steve Torrington, Dave Sheppard, Brian Jackson, Alan Pinnock, Richard Jones and all the staff at the *Daily Mail*.

Thanks also to
Vicki Harris, Peter Wright, Trevor Bunting and Simon Taylor, John Dunne and Kate Truman.

CONTENTS

Introduction

Above: "Beatlemania" entered the English language in November 1963. In the following seven years the Beatles made an extraordinary impact on the world, the reverberations and echoes of which are being felt to the present day.

Opposite: The Beatles in Washington, D.C., before performing their U.S. debut concert at the Coliseum. "I Want To Hold Your Hand" had jumped forty-three places to top the American singles charts.

The fascination of the Beatles' story is not so much their well-documented rise to the top, but how they retained their pre-eminence. They moved on and the fans went with them. The music became increasingly sophisticated and innovative, such that the Beatles would come to be mentioned in the same breath as Beethoven and Schubert.

In January 1962 the Beatles were passed over by popular record label Decca, who offered a recording contract to Brian Poole and the Tremeloes instead, believing that they had the greater potential. Regulars at Liverpool's Cavern Club, where the Beatles had built up a cult following over the previous year, knew that Decca had miscalculated badly. And in 1963 it was confirmed as one of the worst-ever commercial decisions as Beatlemania broke out, first in Britain, then the rest of the world. "From Me to You" gave the Fab Four their first U.K. No.1 in April, and by the end of the year the Beatles had spent eighteen weeks at the top of the charts. Their debut album, *Please Please Me*, went to No. 1 on May 11 and stayed there until December 7—when the group's second offering, *With The Beatles*, took over. It was one of the biggest explosions in pop-music history.

Some were already waiting for the bubble to burst. In January 1964, the Dave Clark Five's "Glad All Over" knocked "I Want To Hold Your Hand" out of the top spot in the U.K., and some were

confidently predicting that the vibrant, stomping London sound would take over from the Mersey Beat as the next big thing. But after mastering the three-minute, three-chord pop song, the Beatles moved on. The albums *Rubber Soul* and *Revolver* were revelations in their range and complexity. The latter was released in August 1966, the month in which the group gave their last concert, at Candlestick Park in San Francisco.

In 1967, the group saw the release of the ground-breaking concept album *Sgt. Pepper*, in which they scaled new creative heights. This seminal work is widely regarded as the greatest rock album of all time. Four short years since the mop-tops shook to "yeah, yeah, yeah" and the girls screamed and fainted in droves, Lennon and McCartney were now considered two of the greatest musical minds of a generation.

The two single releases of 1968, "Lady Madonna" and "Hey Jude," both went to No. 1, as did the double album *The Beatles*, whose stark white cover gave it its more popular name. But the cracks were beginning to show. John and Yoko Ono were now inseparable, the creative tensions were growing, and the band members began working in isolation. January 1969 saw the Beatles' final public performance, a forty-minute set on the roof of the Apple building in Savile Row, London. "Get Back" was the highlight, and on April 23 it became the Beatles sixteenth U.K. No. 1. The seventeenth and last came two months later. Only Lennon and McCartney featured on "The Ballad of John and Yoko," yet another indication that the end was near.

With their business affairs in chaos, the four convened for a glorious swansong album, *Abbey Road*. The studio sessions of early 1969 came to fruition the following year and "Let It Be" was released on March 14, 1970. By the time the album, and film of the same name, came out in May, the Beatles were no more. It was Paul who jumped first, although any of the four could have precipitated the split. John had already had three solo hits by this time, while George had walked out early in 1969, albeit briefly. None of the group attended the premiere of the film, in which the discord between them was plain for all to see.

Ahead lay more wrangling and resentment, particularly over the winding up of their business affairs. But over the decade the Beatles had produced a body of work that was timeless and peerless. It was a golden legacy, one which existing fans could treasure and which succeeding generations would have the unalloyed joy of discovering.

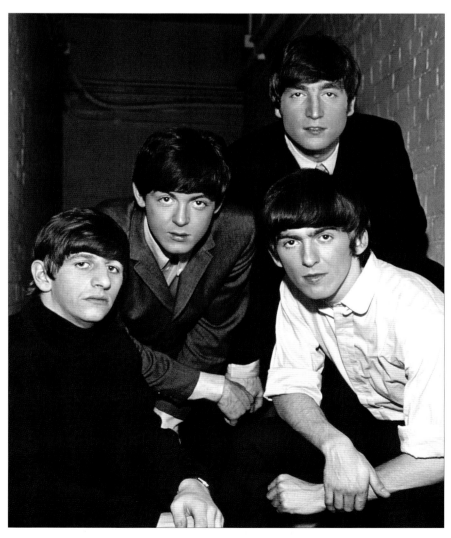

Chapter One

Come Together

Above: The Beatles' performance at the Palais Ballroom in Aldershot, Hampshire, on December 9, 1961, was their first in the south of England. The date was unadvertised and only eighteen people turned up! Left to right: George Harrison, John Lennon, Paul McCartney, and drummer Pete Best. It was not until August 1962 that Ringo Starr replaced Best.

Opposite: Paul engrossed in the latest news on the music scene. "There is no such thing as a Liverpool sound," proclaimed record producer George Martin. "I prefer to talk of the Beatles' sound."

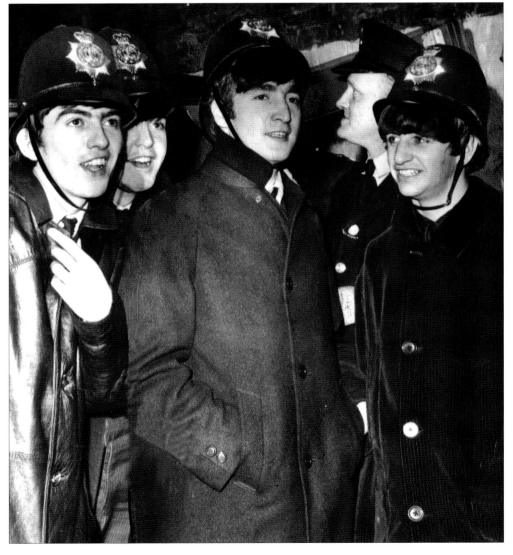

Above: October 17, 1962. The Beatles make their first TV appearance, on *People And Places*, where they perform their debut single, "Love Me Do," along with "Some Other Guy." George Martin had wanted the group to record "How Do You Do It?" for their first single release but they insisted on a self-penned number. "Love Me Do" peaked at No. 17, the only Beatles single which failed to reach the U.K. Top Ten, but it gave them their big breakthrough. Epstein subsequently offered "How Do You Do It?" to Gerry and the Pacemakers, who took it to the top of the U.K. chart in April 1963.

Left: Style wasn't always their first consideration: the band are very thinly disguised as police officers in order to get past the huge crowds gathering for a concert in Birmingham.

Above: While the Fab Four concentrated on songwriting and performing, others played a big part in developing their image. Photographer Astrid Kirchherr—girlfriend of former Beatles bass player Stu Sutcliffe—was responsible for the mop-top hairstyle, a look they adopted during their Hamburg days. Manager Brian Epstein, a former drama student, was also interested in the group's stage presentation. Leather was out, replaced by smart matching suits, and gigs ended with a deep bow to the audience. The importance Epstein placed on image wasn't matched by an awareness of its commercial value; the merchandising contracts he entered into cost the group millions of dollars.

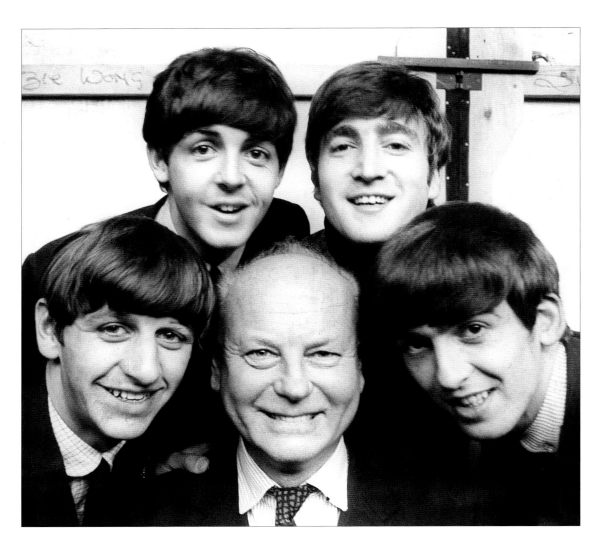

eft: The Beatles' appeal crossed the generation gap; moms and dads became fans as well as the kids. Here, veteran British writer and broadcaster Godfrey Winn poses with the hottest property in showbusiness.

Above: October 13, 1963. Anxious looks from John, Paul and road manager Neil Aspinall as they try to dodge the fans after a barnstorming set on the network variety show *Sunday Night at the London Palladium*. Aspinall and other members of the entourage regularly signed publicity photos to give to fans, as the Beatles themselves couldn't hope to keep up with the ever-increasing demand.

Opposite bottom: In November 1963, the Fab Four's exhausting recording and performing schedule left little time for relaxation. Model car racing was a popular diversion between shows, and John even had a track set up at home.

Above: The Beatles round off a memorable year with an appearance on the supremely popular *Morecambe and Wise Show*. On December 7, 1963, *With The Beatles* replaced *Please Please Me* at the top of the charts and became the U.K.'s first million-selling album. Together, these two albums would put the Beatles at No. 1 for fifty-one consecutive weeks. On the singles front, "I Want To Hold Your Hand" took over the top spot from "She Loves You" on December 12, giving the group three No. 1 singles for the year. Lennon-McCartney were able to claim a fourth success, having also written "Bad to Me," which Billy J. Kramer and the Dakotas took to the top of the charts in August.

Opposite: October 31, 1963. There is chaos at London Airport as the Beatles return from a week-long sell-out tour of Sweden, the group's first overseas booking as healiner and a far cry from the days of near-destitution in Hamburg. Prime Minister Sir Alec Douglas-Home, who happened to be at the airport at the same time, was among those who witnessed the hysteria firsthand.

The Beatles in costume during rehearsals for their Christmas show at Finsbury Park Astoria, London, which included a mix of music, sketches and pantomime. *Life* magazine was preparing a feature on pop's latest phenomenon and had decided to put the group on the cover of the January 31, 1964, issue. The boys turned up at the Astoria too late for the photo-shoot and thus missed out on what was regarded as the most prestigious honor journalism could offer.

ight: John signing copies of *With The Beatles*. Its cover, a monochrome portrait of the four in half-light, shot by Robert Freeman, would become an iconic image of the era. EMI hated it, thinking it drab and humorless, but the group insisted that it be used.

elow: Rehearsing for the Royal Variety Performance, which was held at the Prince of Wales Theater on November 4, 1963. The Beatles stole the show, which was watched by twenty-six million when it was aired on television. They ended their set with "Twist And Shout," John introducing the number in his inimitable, irreverent style: "Will those in the cheaper seats clap your hands; the rest of you just rattle your jewelry." The "ad lib" was planned; the audience, including the Queen Mother, loved it.

Right: January 1964. John and George on their way to Paris, where the Beatles had a three-week, twenty-date booking at the city's Olympia Theater. It wasn't a great success. The Parisian audiences were lukewarm and their response set the tone for the press reviews. Singers Trini Lopez and Sylvie Vartan, who were also on the bill, were given a much better reception.

Opposite top: Café society, mop-top style. The French press may not have been overly impressed with the Beatles but the heavyweight newspapers in England were taking them seriously. Writing in the London *Times*, music critic William Mann hailed Lennon and McCartney as the outstanding English composers of the day. His analysis of their style included phrases such as "flat-submediant key switches." That would have meant little to John and Paul, who wrote instinctively and had limited knowledge of music theory.

Left: Ringo wears his corduroy jacket as the Fab Four arrive for a concert in Huddersfield. Young people everywhere wanted to dress like the Beatles. The struggling corduroy industry experienced a spike in sales during this period as eager fans flocked to stores to acquire the Beatles look.

Above: George, Paul and John take time out from their hectic performing schedule in Paris for a spot of leisurely sightseeing. The fact that France was proving to be one of the tougher markets to crack had one silver lining: they were able to play the tourist role without having to worry about screaming mobs.

Opposite: John and Cynthia prepare to fly to the U.S.A., where Epstein had negotiated top billing on the *Ed Sullivan Show* on successive weeks, February 9 and 16. The fee was a paltry $10,000 but this trip was about exposure, not money. The boys themselves harbored doubts about their ability to crack America, something no British act had managed to do.

Left: The Beatles arrive at New York's Idlewild Airport to the sight and sound of several hundred cheering fans who have gathered to greet the Fab Four.

Right: February 1964. The two concerts at New York's Carnegie Hall were massively over-subscribed and hugely successful, which must have been a great relief to Sid Bernstein, the promoter who had booked them a year earlier. Bernstein hadn't even heard the group play when the deal was done early in 1963, basing his decision entirely on the hype of British press reports. Had the Beatles been a passing craze, it would have been an expensive mistake.

Above: Pau and John hold their guitars on the set of the *Ed Sullivan Show*. An estimated seventy-three million viewers watched the boys perform "All My Loving," "Till There Was You," "She Loves You," "I Saw Her Standing There," and "I Want To Hold Your Hand," which had reached No. 1 on the U.S. Billboard chart a week earlier. It was a vindication and a relief for Capitol Records, EMI's American subsidiary, who had declined to release the group's first four singles.

Right: The Beatles relax with a carriage ride in New York's Central Park before flying to Washington, D.C., to perform at the city's Coliseum Theater.

Above: Cruising off the coast of Miami, from where the second *Ed Sullivan Show* was broadcast. It was another triumph, again attracting an audience of seventy million–plus. The country's police departments had particular cause to be pleased as youth crime all but disappeared for the show's duration.

Opposite top: Taking in the sights of Washington, D.C. There was a lot of hype surrounding the Beatles' Stateside visit. Capitol spent $50,000 on publicity, and there were rumors that high school kids were paid to give them a rapturous welcome on their arrival. Beatlemania proved to be as contagious in the United States as it had been in Britain.

eft: By Beatles' standards, the schedule—three concerts and the two *Ed Sullivan Show* appearances in two weeks—was hardly grueling and left plenty of time for sun, sea, and sand in Miami. "I Want To Hold Your Hand" would still be at No. 1 a month after the boys had returned home, seven weeks in all. The previous year's singles, which hadn't fared well the first time round, then rocketed up the charts. First came "She Loves You," which Capitol had licensed to Swan Records for release in September 1963. It replaced "I Want To Hold Your Hand" at No. 1 on March 21, 1964. However, the greatest coup came two weeks later as the Beatles occupied the top five places in the U.S. singles chart, a feat unmatched before or since. The chart of April 4, 1964, read as follows: 1. "Can't Buy Me Love" 2. "Twist And Shout" 3. "She Loves You" 4. "I Want To Hold Your Hand" 5. "Please Please Me."

Miami, February 18, 1964. The world's greatest group meets its self-proclaimed greatest boxer. That was in fact how it turned out, as Cassius Clay went on to beat Sonny Liston to win the heavyweight championship a week later. However, this was a photo-opportunity the image-conscious Beatles would rather have avoided. Liston was the hot favorite to retain his title and the boys, keen to associate themselves with success, had wanted to meet him instead. It was only after the champion refused that they agreed to meet the brash young challenger.

Right: March 21, 1964. George accompanies actress Hayley Mills to a charity performance of the film *Charade*. Work on the Beatles' own debut movie, *A Hard Day's Night*, had just started. The distinctive chord that opened the title track was played by George on his new twelve-string Rickenbacker, a gift from the manufacturer on the Beatles' recent U.S. tour.

Above: April 1964. Paul and Ringo at Les Ambassadeurs, London, where the nightclub scenes for *A Hard Day's Night* were filmed. The title came courtesy of a throwaway line from Ringo. United Artists' main interest was in the lucrative soundtrack album, which wasn't covered in the group's EMI contract. On general release in July 1964, the film was a huge hit with the critics as well as the fans, receiving two Academy Award nominations. The one sour note was that Epstein was again guilty of poor judgment. The producers were prepared to offer the Beatles twenty-five percent of the profits; they could barely conceal their glee when Epstein said he wouldn't settle for a penny less than seven-and-a-half.

Fan club secretary Bettina Rose helps George to wade through more than fifty sacks of mail as he celebrates his twenty-first birthday. Jelly babies were a popular gift following a newspaper report suggesting he had a weakness for the candy. George, the youngest Beatle, had concentrated his efforts on his guitar playing and had only recently begun to try his hand at songwriting. The first Harrison song to feature on a Beatles album was "Don't Bother Me," on *With The Beatles*. His output increased gradually, and from *Help!* onwards Beatles albums always featured a contribution from George. However, it would not be until 1969, with the release of "Something," that a Harrison song became an A-side single.

Right: These four girls become the envy of millions as they get to run their combs through the most famous hair in the world during the making of *A Hard Day's Night*. Working on George's locks is Pattie Boyd, whom he would marry in January 1966.

Left: March 19, 1964. The Beatles celebrate winning the Variety Club of Great Britain award for 1963 Showbusiness Personalities of the Year. Top politician Harold Wilson presented the award at the luncheon, which was held at London's Dorchester Hotel. Wilson, who would become prime minister in October of that year, was well aware that the Beatles contributed millions to the economy in export earnings.

Chapter Two

Ticket to Ride

Above: George, Paul, and John sing during a concert performance. By 1964 Beatlemania had spread across the globe, and the boys were in high demand. Huge crowds turned out to greet them, not only at concerts, but even when their plane touched down to refuel.

Opposite: Paul pictured during a break in filming *A Hard Day's Night* at Twickenham Studios. He wrote "Can't Buy Me Love," one of the film's two single releases, in Paris between shows at the Olympia Theater. It went to No. 1 in the U.K. on March 26 and in the U.S. a week later. Advance sales worldwide were over two million, an all-time record.

Left: The TV show *Ready Steady Go* gets its biggest audience ever when the Beatles play live in March 1964.

Below: The Beatles pictured with Walter Shenson, producer of *A Hard Day's Night*. United Artists wanted Shenson to bring in a low-budget film to cash in on the group's popularity. Shenson realized that they were no five-minute wonder. He shrewdly cut a deal by which all rights to the film reverted to him after fifteen years.

Opposite: Hamming it up in a spoof version of *A Midsummer Night's Dream*. The sketch formed part of the TV show *Around The Beatles*. Brian Epstein had been concerned about how the boys would sound on TV but had promised they wouldn't be miming to their records. He was as good as his word. For the show's musical interludes the group mimed to a specially recorded set.

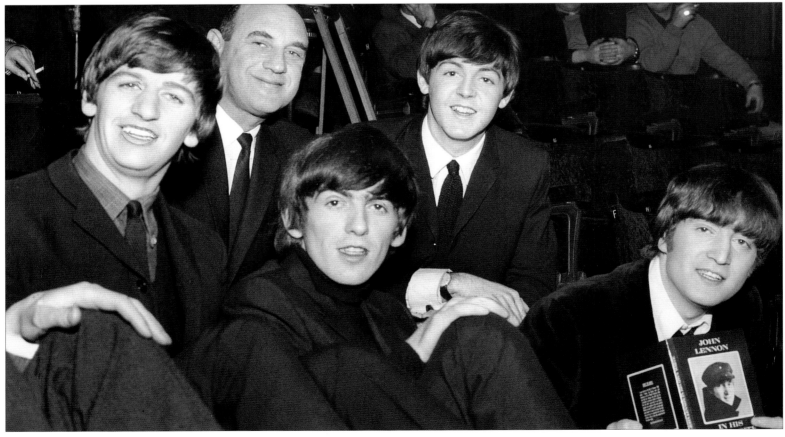

Above: Scotland lays out the welcome mat. The Beatles warm up for their forthcoming world tour by playing two concerts in Edinburgh at the end of April 1964. While the boys were sending the Scottish fans wild, they chalked up yet another first: Ella Fitzgerald became the first artist to chart with a Lennon-McCartney composition, taking "Can't Buy Me Love" to No. 34 in the U.K.

Above and right: The shows in Scotland were rapidly sold out, leaving thousands of disappointed fans out in the street simply hoping to catch a glimpse of their idols. The lucky few got to meet the boys and took away a treasured autograph. The schedule was relentless but there was always time for composing. If Lennon and McCartney had a spare two hours on the road or in a hotel room, they would discipline themselves to write a new song. Although the final credit would be equal, Paul and John often worked on ideas separately before polishing them together.

Left: The Beatles did three shows in Scotland, one in Edinburgh followed by two at the Glasgow Odeon. It wouldn't be long before the adulation of the fans and deafening scenes in the concert halls would begin to wear thin. George would be the first to tire of the trappings that accompanied Beatlemania.

Below: The bland backdrop is a far cry from the theatrical razzmatazz that today's concert-goer would expect. The Beatles phenomenon was all about four good-looking guys who could play and sing great pop songs.

osing for another photo-call before going on stage in Scotland. "Can't Buy Me Love" had just been knocked off the top of the U.K. charts by Peter and Gordon's "World Without Love," which Paul had written as a sixteen-year-old. Ironically, it was deemed inappropriate for the Beatles, so Paul offered it to his girlfriend Jane Asher's brother, Peter Asher. The song was Peter Asher and Gordon Waller's debut single, and reached No. I on both sides of the Atlantic.

Paul and George rehearsing for their performance at the Prince of Wales Theater, London, on Sunday May 11, 1964. The repertoire included "Can't Buy Me Love," "All My Loving," "Roll Over Beethoven," "Till There Was You," "This Boy," "Long Tall Sally," and "Twist And Shout." The show was the fifth in a series of seven Sunday-night pop shows at the theater promoted by Brian Epstein.

Right: May 31, 1964. The boys get together before the show at the Prince of Wales Theater, after vacationing separately for a few weeks. The touring schedule for the rest of the year is announced, beginning in Denmark on June 4. This would be followed by a trip to Australia and a return visit to the U.S.A. Five U.K. dates were also penciled in to keep the home fans happy.

Left: Even the Beatles need to run through their set prior to their world tour. While the boys were practicing, "Love Me Do" finally made it to No. 1 in the U.S., some eighteen months after it had charted in the U.K. When the song was recorded, in September 1962, producer George Martin had been unhappy with Ringo's drumming and arranged for a session musician to replace him on some of the takes. Ringo played on the U.K. release, but the U.S. version featured the session drummer.

Left and below: Whether it was toasting the success of forthcoming tours or post-concert winding down, the booze always flowed freely. The Beatles had not experimented with marijuana yet, though; it is said that Bob Dylan introduced them to pot during their second visit to the U.S., in August 1964.

Above: In Elizabethan costume for *Around the Beatles*, the first British TV show built entirely around the famous quartet. The hour-long spectacular was broadcast on May 6, 1964.

Left: June 3, 1964. Ringo is laid low with tonsillitis the day before the Beatles embark on their world tour. Jimmy Nicol, a respected session drummer who had also played with Georgie Fame and the Blue Flames is catapulted into the spotlight as Ringo's replacement. He had little time to practice the new material at EMI Studios before the airplane left for Denmark.

Jimmy Nicol would play the first five dates of the tour, a recovered Ringo taking over in Australia. Nicol received £500 and a gold watch for his services before slipping back into relative obscurity. In his brief time as a Beatle he did make one significant contribution: when asked how he was coping, Nicol's stock reply was "It's getting better." Almost three years later Paul would use this as an inspiration for a song on *Sgt. Pepper*.

aul shows off a traditional memento from the Dutch leg of the world tour. Although this was the group's most grueling performing schedule thus far, there was still time for writing and recording. As well as *A Hard Day's Night*, which was about to hit the record shops and movie theaters, there would be another No. 1 single and album before the year was over. *Beatles For Sale* would feature eight new Lennon-McCartney songs. The single "I Feel Fine," which topped the chart in December 1964, was not featured on the album. This was a deliberate decision on the part of the group, who felt that this common practice represented poor value for the fans.

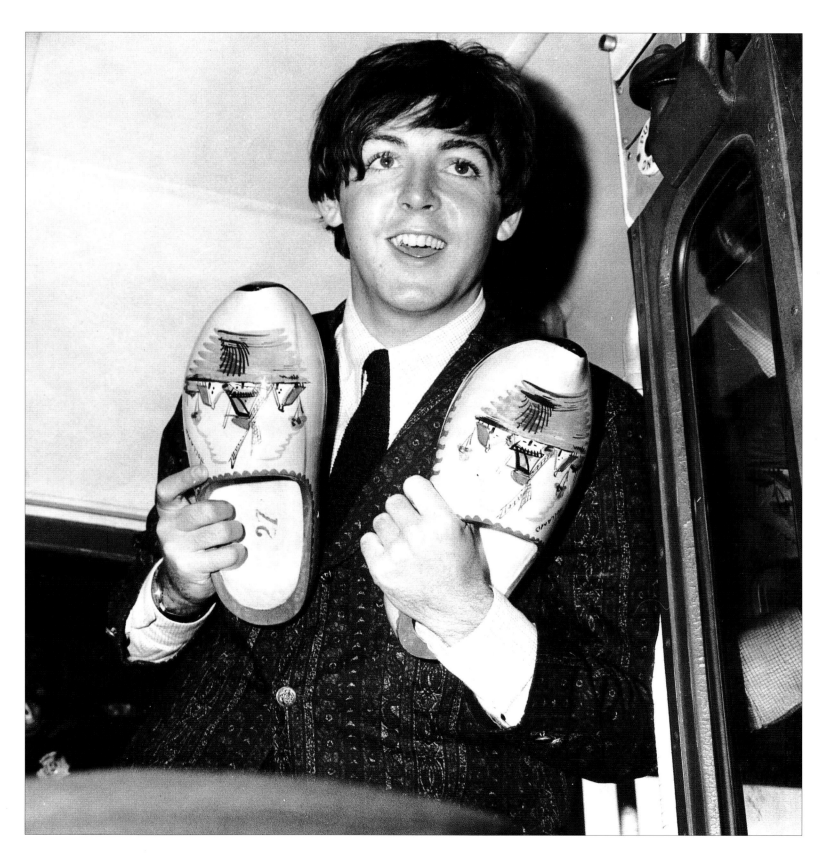

rriving back from a staggeringly successful tour of Europe, the Far East, and Australia. The Australians saw some of the most remarkable scenes, eclipsing anything seen in Britain and America. Crowds of over 250,000 greeted the boys in Melbourne and Adelaide, said to be the largest ever gathering of Australians in one place.

Left: The nightclub scene from *A Hard Day's Night*. The film received its world premiere on July 6, 1964. The soundtrack album was the first to feature exclusively Beatles compositions.

Below: A city honors its own. Four days after the London premiere of *A Hard Day's Night*, the Beatles attend a special screening of the movie in Liverpool and are also guests of honor at a civic reception at the city's town hall. An estimated 200,000-strong crowd lined the route from Speke Airport (later renamed John Lennon Airport) to the city center.

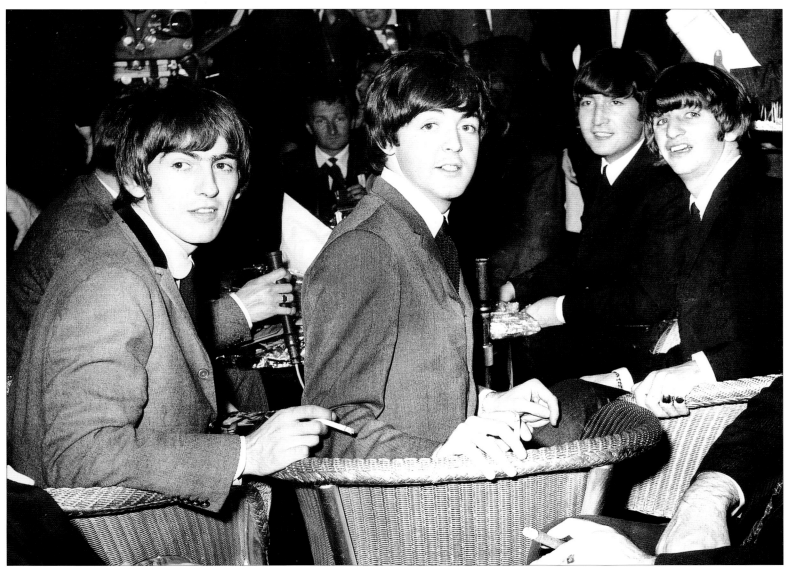

The Beatles meet Princess Margaret at the premiere of *A Hard Day's Night*. It is said that the humming of Beatles tunes was regularly heard in the royal palaces. The soundtrack album went to the top of the U.K. chart on July 25 and stayed there until December 19—when it was supplanted by *Beatles For Sale*. As far as the film was concerned, what started out as a low-budget exploitation movie became a classic of its genre. Universally lauded for its wit and style, it took in $8 million during its first week. Subsequent movie projects would not be so well received.

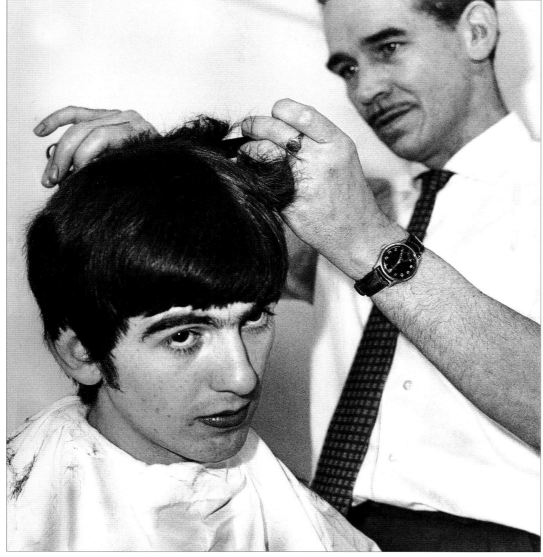

Above: When the Beatles weren't on stage they were invariably in hotels, at airports, or making personal appearances. Their astonishing productivity had already made them serious money, particularly John and Paul for their songwriting. They were advised to set up their own company, Northern Songs, but this was merely a subsidiary of a larger corporate empire. This was to have dire consequences, artistic as well as financial; it meant that Lennon and McCartney didn't own their own songs.

Left: Every aspect of a Beatle's life was of interest to the fans and here George is photographed having his hair cut.

Left: The Beatles appear in the variety show *Blackpool Night Out.* Although 1964 was the year in which the group became a worldwide phenomenon, there was still ample opportunity for the home fans to see them play live. There were five concerts at seaside resorts during the summer, and a U.K. tour was scheduled for the fall. The latter included a gig at the Liverpool Empire, the first time the boys had played in their home city in almost a year.

Above: The Beatles line up with the rest of the bill for *Blackpool Night Out.* Just a year earlier the boys had had to plead with headline star Roy Orbison for permission to close the show in which they both appeared. Now there was no act—not even Elvis—who was a bigger draw.

Above: Waving the U.S. fans goodbye at New York's Kennedy Airport in September 1964. The tour took in twenty-four cities in barely a month, the entourage clocking up more than twenty thousand miles. Kansas City wasn't part of the itinerary but a local millionaire was determined that the group play there. He got his wish, but at a cost of $150,000—a world-record fee for a concert performance—and the set lasted barely half an hour.

Left: George Martin, the EMI A&R man who became known as the fifth Beatle. Martin, a classically trained oboist, had made comedy records with the Goons and also worked with Cilla Black, Gerry and the Pacemakers, and Billy J. Kramer. But it was as producer of the Beatles' records that he is best known.

Above: Baby, I can drive my car. Twenty-four-year-old John passes his driving test after just seven hours' practice behind the wheel. George, Paul, and Ringo offer their congratulations as John tries George Martin's car for size in the EMI Studios parking lot. Inevitably, expensive cars and property would be among the trappings of success. In 1965 Paul was driving round in an Aston Martin DB4, and also spent £40,000 on the purchase of a house in Cavendish Avenue, St John's Wood, in London. John and Ringo would take up residence in Weybridge, part of Surrey's stockbroker belt.

Opposite: Another Christmas so it must be *Another Beatles Christmas Show*, which opened at London's Hammersmith Odeon on December 24 and ran until mid-January. "I Feel Fine" was at No. 1 in the U.K. singles chart during that period. The distinctive feedback noise which started the song was discovered by accident, after John stood his guitar against an amplifier. They liked the sound so much that they asked George Martin to incorporate it in the track. The group would become increasingly experimental and innovative, lyrically as well as musically.

A bove: February 22, 1965. Legions of screaming fans bid the Beatles farewell as they leave for the
Bahamas, where filming of their second movie was due to begin. Just about all the songs to be used
in the film had already been recorded. The only thing missing was the title track. John and Paul
weren't keen on the working title, *Eight Arms To Hold You*, not least because they thought it awkward
as a lyric. Once *Help!* was settled upon, the duo quickly came up with a typically catchy title song.

A bove: Filming began almost immediately after the crew arrived. On February 23, 1965, all four Beatles were filmed swimming, while fully clothed, in the pool at the Nassau Beach Hotel in the West Bay area.

L eft: Paul gets distracted while bicycling in *Help!* This scene was filmed near the airport on the 21-mile-long island of New Providence in the Bahamas.

Above: The second Beatles feature film again had Dick Lester as director, but the script lacked the wit and sharpness that Alun Owen had given to *A Hard Day's Night*. It would be another box-office success—the seven Beatles songs and the exotic locations saw to that—but *Help!* wasn't very well received by the critics.

Opposite top left: With the filming of *Help!* complete, John and Cynthia fly out to the Cannes Film Festival to see what else is new in the movie world. John was also furthering his literary career. Following the success of his first book, *In His Own Write*, he had just completed *A Spaniard in the Works*, published in July 1965. Wordplay was a Lennon-McCartney trademark and it also featured in the current Beatles chart-topper, "Ticket to Ride": Paul had relatives who ran a bar in Ryde, on the Isle of Wight.

Above and below: After the glamor of the Caribbean and Austria, it's back to a chilly England to complete the filming of *Help!*. The album track chosen to feature Ringo on vocals this time around was "Act Naturally," one of only two songs on *Help!* not composed by one of the Beatles.

Above: June 12, 1965. The Beatles become the first pop group featured in the Queen's Birthday Honors list. Paul's initial reaction is a big thumbs up, but the awarding of the Member of the Order of the British Empire (MBE) to the band members was not universally popular. Many existing award holders returned their medals to Buckingham Palace as a protest against a perceived debasing of the honor.

Opposite: Paul is raised aloft as he celebrates his twenty-third birthday on June 18, 1965. It could just as easily have been in recognition of one of his latest compositions, "Yesterday," which would become one of the most popular and most covered of all Beatles songs. Paul woke one morning with the tune in his head. He initially thought it was a melody he had heard somewhere, and it was only after some extensive checking that he claimed it as his own. He needed three syllables for the opening line and used "Scrambled Eggs" as a stopgap until the more poignant lyrics were written.

There was increasing speculation that Paul would become the third Beatle to tie the knot. His relationship with Jane Asher would continue, off and on, for almost another three years. In that time there would be periods of physical separation, particularly as Jane's theater work took her away. There was also a cultural divide: Jane and her circle did not embrace the drug scene in the way that Paul did.

Above: George, Cynthia, John, Ringo, and Maureen attend the world premiere of *Help!* at the London Pavilion. The album topped the chart on both sides of the Atlantic, as did the title track. In September 1965 "Yesterday" was released as a single in the U.S.A., with "Act Naturally" on the flipside. That too made it to No. 1, the eighth Beatles song to do so. This equaled the group's achievement at home.

Left: John is in clowning mode as the Beatles return home at the end of a nine-date European tour. The pose reflects the fact that they had just played Barcelona, or perhaps it was a subtle plug for his new book.

ight: Paul and Ringo on their way to Buckingham Palace to receive their MBEs. En route it's just a cigarette; later it will be marijuana in one of the royal lavatories.

pposite: Following the investiture ceremony the boys show off their latest awards, with Brian Epstein proudly looking on. Unsurprisingly, it was John who came closest to refusing the honor. While he was loath to be regarded as an establishment figure, both Paul and the group's manager were overjoyed. Ironically, the fact that the award outraged a number of military men helped to change John's mind. If others could be given a medal for killing people, he pointed out, then the Beatles surely deserved theirs for entertaining them.

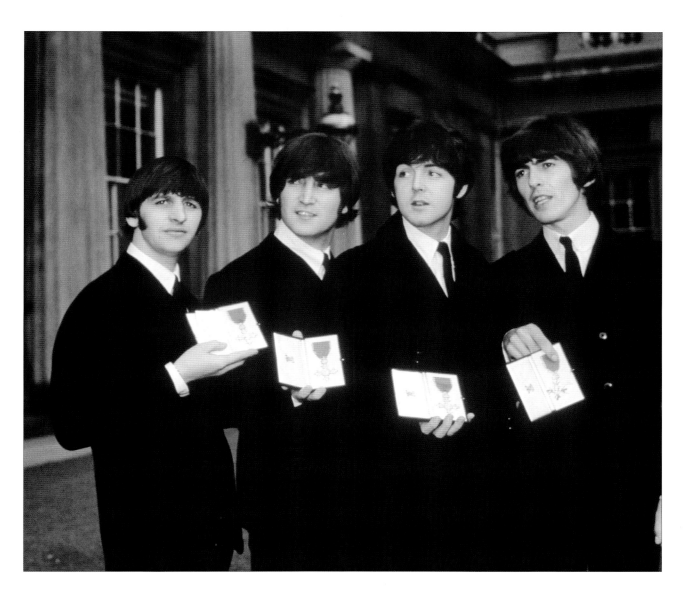

ight: New dad gets a new beard. An even more hirsute Ringo leaves for a short Caribbean holiday with Maureen, January 1966. Son Zak had been born on September 13 the previous year. *Rubber Soul*, released in December 1965, gave Ringo his first writing credit. He maintained he made a minimal contribution to "What Goes On," one of the fourteen new songs that made up the album. *Rubber Soul* would be seen as the start of a new phase in the group's career, its songs showing greater diversity and complexity than previous releases.

Opposite and above: George and Pattie marry with Paul doing the honors as best man on January 21, 1966, at Esher Register Office. Pattie's Mary Quant fox fur coat was a wedding present from George. Her gift to him was a set of George III wine goblets. The two left for a honeymoon in Barbados with the Beatles yet again at the top of both the singles and album charts. The double A-side "Day Tripper/We Can Work It Out" gave the group their third Christmas No. 1 in a row. *Rubber Soul* included two Harrison songs, "Think For Yourself" and "If I Needed Someone." Perhaps of more significance was his sitar playing on "Norwegian Wood," the first trace of an Eastern influence on the Beatles' music.

Opposite: May 1, 1966. The Beatles give what is to be their last British performance, at the NME Poll Winners' Concert, held at the Empire Pool, Wembley, north London. A contractual dispute meant that cameras failed to capture the fifteen-minute set which included "I Feel Fine," "Nowhere Man," "Day Tripper," "If I Needed Someone," and "I'm Down." The luster of live shows was now wearing thin, and as Beatles' music was becoming increasingly sophisticated its natural home was the studio.

Above: An appearance on *Top of the Pops* is a milestone for any British performer, even the Beatles. Here, they rehearse for their set, which included both sides of their new single, "Paperback Writer" and "Rain." The former featured complex harmonies and Paul playing lead bass; the latter included backward guitar and was the group's first overtly psychedelic track.

On June 24, 1966, the Beatles depart for West Germany, the first leg in a tour that also took in Japan and the Philippines. There was a rapturous welcome in Hamburg, where they visited for the first time since playing at the Star Club in December 1962. The adulation meant little by now, and touring had become a chore. By contrast, the studio work on their new album was breaking new ground. *Revolver*, released in August 1966, would represent a new high-water mark in Beatles music.

Left and below: A relieved foursome arrives back in London and holds a press conference after a harrowing experience in the Philippines. The two shows in Manila on July 4 went down well with the eighty thousand who managed to get a ticket. However, things turned nasty when Brian Epstein decided that they wouldn't attend a reception organized by the president's wife, Imelda Marcos. It was construed as a deliberate snub, and the following morning an angry mob gave the group and their entourage a hostile send-off at Manila Airport.

Right: August 11, 1966. Almost the end of the road as far as touring is concerned. The Beatles leave for America, where they fly into another storm. Lennon's comment that the Beatles were "more popular than Jesus" created few waves when it appeared in the London *Evening Standard* five months earlier. The reaction was very different when the transcript of the interview was printed in an American magazine just before the group's arrival in the States. The Bible Belt was outraged. Beatles records were publicly burned and death threats were issued. Lennon defused the situation with an apology but this was the last straw for the Beatles and touring. On August 29 at Candlestick Park, San Francisco, they gave their final concert performance.

Left and opposite: Fall 1966 saw John make a brief return to acting. In September he began filming *How I Won The War*, Dick Lester's black comedy in which he played Private Gripweed. It was on location in Spain that he wrote "Strawberry Fields Forever." In November he donned a doorman's uniform for a sketch in Peter Cook and Dudley Moore's TV program *Not Only ... But Also*. He played the doorman of a "Members Only" men's restroom for the show, which aired on December 26, 1966. But for Lennon the most significant event of this period took place on November 9: that was the day he visited an exhibition at the Indica Gallery, London, where he met underground artist Yoko Ono for the first time.

Chapter Three

Hello Goodbye

above: Ringo joins the Harrisons on a vacation in Athens in July 1967, leaving a heavily pregnant Maureen at home. The military junta which had recently seized control was keen to use the visit for tourism and propaganda purposes. The Beatles toyed with the idea of setting up a commune on a Greek island, but the idea was quickly abandoned.

Opposite: With *Sgt. Pepper's Lonely Hearts Club Band* at No. 1 on the U.K. album chart, where it would remain for six months, the Beatles take part in the first global TV broadcast, *Our World*. An estimated audience of 400 million watched the group perform "All You Need Is Love," composed specially for the event. It would become the anthem of the "Summer of Love," reaching No. 1 on both sides of the Atlantic. As far as the U.K. chart was concerned, it was a case of normal service being resumed as their previous single, the double A-side "Strawberry Fields Forever"/"Penny Lane," had only reached No. 2. The intervention of Engelbert Humperdinck's "Release Me" meant that the group had their first "failure" at home since "Please Please Me" in 1963.

Above: Back in England after the abortive attempt to set up a hippie commune on a Greek island. One of the main attractions of the idea had been the freedom to indulge in drug-taking without having to fear the long arm of the law. On July 24, 1967, the Beatles signed their names on a full-page advertisement in the London *Times* calling for the reform of Britain's cannabis law. Brian Epstein was also a signatory, but this was little more than a gesture of hanging onto the group's shirttails; he was now becoming an increasingly marginalized figure.

Opposite: The early months of 1967 saw Paul working flat out on *Sgt. Pepper*. Jane Asher, meanwhile, was on tour in America with the Bristol Old Vic theater company. The relationship was stagnating. "I'm Looking Through You," written by Paul for the *Rubber Soul* album, was about a relationship that was more veneer than substance, a thinly veiled sideswipe at Jane and her theatrical ambitions.

Paul and Jane Asher, with four-year-old Julian Lennon. Paul had met photographer Linda Eastman on May 15, 1967, at the Bag o' Nails club in London, and they renewed their acquaintance at the *Sgt. Pepper* launch party four days later. Even so, his unsteady relationship with Jane would continue for several more months.

The Lennons and the Harrisons pay a visit to the Apple Boutique, where beautiful people could buy beautiful things. The Beatles already owned the site, 94 Baker Street, which had been acquired on their behalf for investment purposes. The boutique itself was a personal indulgence and a commercial disaster. It opened in December 1967; within eight months it had lost more than £200,000.

Left: February 1968. Two months after announcing their engagement, Paul and Jane Asher join the other Beatles in Rishikesh for a Transcendental Meditation course run by the Maharishi Mahesh Yogi. The four experienced different levels of enlightenment. Ringo and Maureen had had enough after just two weeks, Paul and Jane lasted five, while the Lennons and the Harrisons stayed for two months. It was a productive songwriting period. Paul's compositions included "Back in the USSR" and "Ob-La-Di, Ob-La-Da." John wrote "Across the Universe" and "Dear Prudence." The latter was written as a plea to Prudence Farrow, sister of actress Mia, who had suffered an anxiety attack and refused to emerge from her quarters.

Right: The bus for *Magical Mystery Tour* proved too wide for this narrow bridge in the Devon countryside. The sixty-seater yellow-and-blue coach, carrying the Beatles and a film crew and decorated in technicolor livery, had to drive in reverse for half a mile and the group had to reconsider their route.

ight: Paul had been the driving creative force behind *Sgt. Pepper* and had already planned the next major Beatles' project, a free-form film without a script. The idea was conceived in April 1967, but apart from recording the title song, "Magical Mystery Tour," it lay dormant for several months. Following the death of Brian Epstein on August 27, Paul moved quickly to get the project off the ground.

eft: John on location while filming *Magical Mystery Tour.* The basis of the project was that they should pile into a bus with a film crew and various other passengers, and just drive around England filming the adventures they were sure to have. The resulting television show was savagely criticized. It has since been the view that critics of the time did not make enough allowances for the experimental nature of the film. By the time the program was released the Beatles had moved on and saw themselves as businessmen, building an empire of which they would take total control.

Beatles and Co., set up in May 1967, was an attempt by the group to take greater control of their affairs. Early the following year it became Apple Corps, a more typically playful corporate name. They were advised that an umbrella company, with subsidiaries for music, film, merchandising and the like, made sound financial sense. The philosophy was to help people help themselves—something which many visitors to the Apple Boutique took all too literally. Predictably, the music division, with artists such as Mary Hopkin and James Taylor, as well as the Beatles themselves, made a healthy profit from the start. "Hey Jude" was the group's first release on the Apple label, reaching No. 1 in the U.K. on September 11, 1968.

Right: By 1968 the Beatles was very much Paul's group. John was in a drug-induced torpor much of the time, leaving Paul to take the initiative and give the band direction. There were plaudits for the seminal *Sgt. Pepper*, but he also had to face the brickbats over *Magical Mystery Tour*, which was panned by the critics. Even John weighed in with a savage condemnation of the project.

Left: Amid scenes reminiscent of the height of Beatlemania, the Apple Boutique closes its doors for the last time, with all remaining stock given away on July 31, 1968.

Opposite: July 1968. John returns to his art college roots by holding an exhibition at the Robert Fraser Gallery in London. It is entitled *You Are Here* and consists of a display of charity boxes. He dedicates the exhibition to Yoko Ono, from whom he is now virtually inseparable. John's numerous LSD trips made him particularly receptive to the ideas and thoughts of the avant-garde artist he first met in November 1966. In Yoko Ono John had finally found a kindred spirit. Life with Cynthia in suburbia was over, as she herself recognized when she filed for divorce in August 1968. John's relationship with the other Beatles was also affected dramatically; his insistence on bringing Ono to recording sessions caused much resentment.

Above: In October John and Yoko are charged with possession of cannabis at Marylebone Court and remanded on bail until November 28. John claims his drug-taking days are over as he is fined £150 for possession of cannabis. The charges against Yoko are dropped.

Left: John and Yoko Ono, with five-year-old Julian Lennon, at a rehearsal for the Rolling Stones' *Rock and Roll Circus*. A host of stars was lined up to perform various circus acts, but the show never made it to the TV screens. More successful was *The Beatles*, the group's eponymous latest release. *The White Album*, as it would come to be known, was an artistic triumph that some felt even eclipsed *Sgt. Pepper*. However, the cracks were beginning to show during recording and it was an album born of individual accomplishment rather than harmonious collaboration.

Left: February 13, 1969. Paul and Linda Eastman at a launch party for Mary Hopkin's debut album *Postcard*. It would reach No. 3 in the U.K. chart, her only successful album release. Many thought Paul and Linda's relationship would be equally short-lived.

Below: Recording at Twickenham Studios, January 1969. With the rifts widening and Apple descending deeper into the mire, Paul made a last-ditch bid to keep the band together. Of the four, he was the one most in love with being a Beatle, and his idea for salvation was that they should go back to their roots, doing what they did best. By the time these filmed performances hit the cinema screens in May 1970, as *Let It Be*, the Beatles were no more.

Above: March 12, 1969. The speculation ends as Paul and Linda marry at Marylebone Register Office, London. Paul had already met the in-laws: a month earlier Linda's father, New York lawyer Lee Eastman, had been appointed to help sort out Apple Corps, which was now in total disarray. The other Beatles were suspicious, and insisted that Eastman's firm work under their man, Allen Klein.

Right: Naturally the press were keen to relate the story of the woman who had captivated the last bachelor Beatle. It was revealed that during her time at the University of Arizona she had been briefly married to a fellow student, by whom she had daughter Heather, now six. They were wide of the mark in claiming that she was an heiress to the Eastman-Kodak fortune, a myth that persisted despite her repeated denials.

Opposite: George and Pattie Harrison appear at Esher and Walton Magistrates' Court on a charge of cannabis possession. The £250 fine was a drop in the ocean compared to the millions that had gone astray in the Beatles' corporate dealings. George had briefly walked out on the group during the *Let It Be* recording sessions. Eastern music and philosophy would more than fill the void left by the break-up of the band. George had been the first to become disenchanted with life as a Beatle and was now probably the least committed to the group's survival.

Left: John and Yoko often mirrored each other in their choice of attire. John went one stage further, by legally changing his name to John Ono Lennon. The ceremony took place on the roof of the Apple building on April 22, 1969, just one month after their wedding in Gibraltar. This was where the Beatles had played a celebrated forty-minute set on January 30, the group's final public performance.

Eight days after Paul and Linda's wedding, John and Yoko Ono marry in the British Consulate building, Gibraltar. A seven-day bed-in at the Amsterdam Hilton follows, which is recorded for posterity in the lyrics of "The Ballad of John and Yoko." Although neither John nor Paul invited the other to attend his wedding, there was an element of old-style collaboration on the song. John had it mostly worked out; Paul helped him complete it. With George away and Ringo busy filming *The Magic Christian*, John and Paul between them did all the vocals and played all the instruments. It was to be the Beatles' last U.K. No. 1, topping the chart in June 1969. In the U.S. it only reached No. 8 as some radio stations took exception to the line "Christ, you know it ain't easy" and refused to give it air play.

While many of John and Yoko's avant-garde ideas left people bemused, "Give Peace a Chance," recorded by the two of them and an assortment of acquaintances as the Plastic Ono Band, had more commercial appeal. It reached No. 2 in the U.K. in July 1969, John's first chart success without the other Beatles.

A bove: Even with the help of Linda's father and Allen Klein, the Beatles continued to lose money through their corporation. Here, Paul leaves the Apple offices after more discussions about the future of Apple Corps.

R ight: George returns from a vacation in Sardinia. Tensions among the band members finally erupted during rehearsal sessions for *Get Back* in January 1969, and George temporarily left the band, only to return a few days later.

An evening out in London. There is also a happy event to look forward to; Linda, four months pregnant when they married, would give birth to Mary on August 28, 1969.

ight: George is perfectly at home among members of London's Radha Krishna Temple, a Hindu sect that advocates self-purification. Alcohol, drugs, and recreational sex—the staple diet of rock'n' rollers—were banned. That didn't stop them having a Top 20 single in September 1969, "Hare Krishna Mantra," the unlikeliest hit of the year. George himself would be the first of the Beatles to have a solo No. 1 when "My Sweet Lord" topped the charts in 1971.

eft: John's espousal of love and freedom finds an outlet as he takes up the case of James Hanratty, who was convicted of Britain's infamous "A6 murder" in 1961 and hanged the following year. He and Yoko meet Hanratty's parents, who continue to declare their son's innocence. John was in a much less charitable mood when he discovered that Paul had been buying shares in Apple behind the other Beatles' backs.

Right: February 1971. Paul and Linda pictured during the nine-day High Court hearing to dissolve Beatles & Co. Paul found that his only recourse was to sue the other three band members, an act which went down badly with the fans. The man who had done more than anyone to keep the Beatles together in the latter years was inevitably cast in the role of villain, responsible for breaking up the greatest group of all time. Legally, the end came in January 1975, long after the four had gone their separate ways.

Below: In October 1971 John released *Imagine* to great critical acclaim. It went to No. 1, equaling the success of McCartney's second album, *Ram*, four months earlier. The ill-feeling between the two continued in some of the lyrics of their solo songs, such as McCartney's "Too Many People" and Lennon's "How Do You Sleep?."

On March 31, 1972, the Official Beatles Fan Club closed down. Hopes of a reconciliation continued among fans for the next eight years, until Lennon was shot and killed outside the Dakota building in New York City on December 8, 1980. The dream of all four Beatles playing together again was over; a matchless and timeless canon of work remained.

Epilogue

From the moment the Beatles went their separate ways, their legions of fans entertained hopes of a reconciliation. The acrimonious legal wrangling was not settled until 1975, however, and by then the four had established themselves as solo artists.

Paul enjoyed huge success with his new band, Wings, notably with the 1973 album *Band on the Run* and the 1977 single "Mull of Kintyre," which replaced "She Loves You" as the U.K.'s best-selling single ever. John topped the album charts on both sides of the Atlantic with his 1971 album *Imagine*, but after Yoko gave birth to a son, Sean, in 1975 he decided to take a five-year sabbatical to enjoy fatherhood the second time around. George emerged from the shadows of John and Paul with the acclaimed triple album *All Things Must Pass*, although the hit single "My Sweet Lord" became the subject of a successful plagiarism suit for its similarity to the Chiffons song "He's So Fine." He met his second wife, Olivia Arias, through Dark Horse Records, the label he founded in 1974. Ringo had a string of hit singles, including "Photograph" and "You're Sixteen," and also added to his list of acting credits with films such as *That'll Be the Day*.

When John was gunned down outside the Dakota building by Mark Chapman on December 8, 1980, just after releasing his comeback album *Double Fantasy*, the world mourned the loss of a musical genius who had influenced an entire generation. All hopes that the world's greatest band might re-form were finally dashed.

Paul continued to expand his musical horizons, although when he closed Live Aid in July 1985 he chose a Beatles song, "Let It Be." By then he was officially the most successful composer of all time, with single and album sales topping 200 million.

George helped to form supergroup The Traveling Wilburys in 1988 and also found a creative outlet as a movie producer with his company HandMade films, whose credits included *Time Bandits* and *A Private Function*.

It was on the set of the film *Caveman* that Ringo met his second wife, Barbara Bach. He later relaunched his own musical career by forming the All-Starrs, whose line-up eventually included son Zak.

Linda McCartney lost her fight against cancer in 1998, and three years later, on November 29, 2001, George succumbed to the same disease. Paul married former model Heather Mills in 2002 and continues to play to sell-out audiences. He and Ringo are now the sole bearers of the Beatles' legacy. Although all four members of the group possessed remarkable individual talents, it is for the unique melding of their separate gifts that they will forever be remembered, both in the record books and, more important, in the hearts of music fans the world over.

Index

Fitzgerald, Ella, 38
France, 22, 24
Freeman, Robert, 21
"From Me To You," 10